Powerful Pleasant Peach

69 tips to a healthy Vagina

Feminine Hygiene

This book was written to help women get married and stay married. Unfortunately, in some cases, issues with feminine health can cause relationships to break down. To prevent this from happening in your marriage, I recommend using the following home remedies and preventive methods with wisdom and discretion. Consulting a physician is recommended in the case of any medical emergencies.

These remedies have been used and recommended by myself, friends, colleagues, and family members. It is my hope to learn more about feminine hygiene.

Feminine Hygiene

Introduction

This book was written to help women get married and stay married. I have known women who have had issues with their feminine health at some point in their lives that caused their relationships to breakdown. I wanted to make sure that didn't stop you from having healthy intimacy during marriage. It can be embarrassing to go to the doctor to put your vagina in some doctor's face and have an uncomfortable pap-smear. It is even worse having to discuss it with your partner. I am a Metaphysicist who formerly worked in a traditional medical environment. Use these methods with wisdom and discretion. Consult your physician for medical emergencies. These are home remedies that have been used by myself, friends, colleagues, and family members. I am not giving medical advice. I have seen prolapsed uterus, tons of women have hysterectomies that could have been prevented with education. Marriages and relationships could have been saved if there had been open communication about sex and health. My goal is to get you talking, asking more questions, researching, and sharing with all the women and men in your lives so we produce a healthier society of women.

Fresh Peach

1. Take baths daily and never use bubble bath causes the natural PH of the peach (Vagina) to go out of balance which can cause yeast and bacteria infections. Use plain, unperfumed soaps to wash the area around the vagina gently every day. Spread your lips apart and gently clean around the folds with a clean washcloth or your hands. Remember to avoid getting water or soap inside your vagina. Let the area dry naturally or pat it dry with a towel. Take a bath after sex, exercise, and sweating.

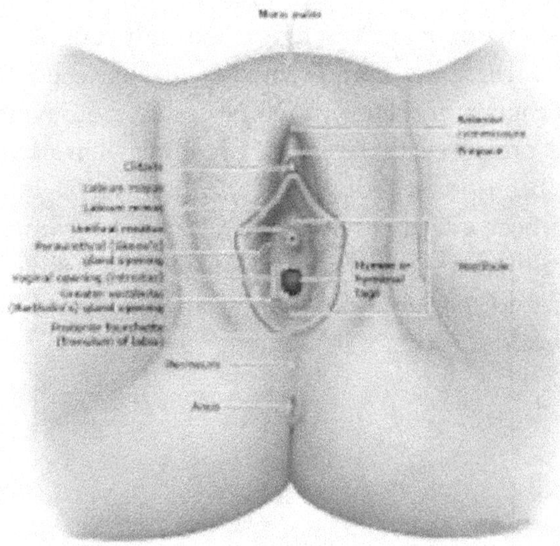

2. Never put soap inside of your vagina. Clean the inside of the labia the two flaps of skin on the vagina with a PH balanced cleanser.

3. Tea baths detox the peach as well as the rest of the body. Let's list a few benefits: detoxification of the skin. Reduces inflammation, and

soothes and softens the texture of your skin. Relaxes irritated muscles and reduces muscle pain/It cleanses your skin as well, while detoxing it also helps to close your pores. Assists with healing sunburn. The antioxidants in the tea are ideal for anti-aging properties. Helps your skin to recover from environmental negative triggers. Some teas like Chamomile are antibacterial, which help immensely with reducing scars and marks all over your body, to name a few benefits. And last but certainly not least, it is also the perfect aromatic "me-time" escape plan :) The herbs in tea pull toxins out the pores of the skin. 1. Tea The best teas for your ultimate soak: Chamomile-When you think about drinking this tea, they are known for their calming, relaxing and soothing abilities. Some people even use this to ease them into sleep. Now imagine your body's largest organ-your skin in the tub soaking with chamomile! A similar phenomenon takes place and after being exposed to harsh sunlight, dry winter conditions, environmental germs and irritants, that's exactly what your skin, mind and senses need. Green Tea-There's a reason this is a popular pick for a tea bath and that's mainly due to its detoxifying agents that help to cleanse and heal the skin. Talk about cleansing from the inside out, now you can join this trend also and your skin will thank you for it later. Black Tea-Let's establish that Black Tea is different from taking a normal tea bag and brewing it without adding milk, that's not it, instead it is a special type of tea that has a higher oxidation concentration than your normal blends, like Yellow, oolong, normal white tea leaves and even green tea. Due to this, it is much stronger in flavor, which makes it perfect for a bath soak. https://shop.totallifechanges.com/ home?lang=en&sponsor=Acooley

4. V steam has been practiced in Africa (Mozambique, South Africa), Asia (Indonesia, Thailand), and Central America (among the Q'eqchi' people). Vaginal steaming is described in spas as an ancient Chinese treatment for reproductive organ ailments and is claimed to have other benefits. It is the practice in which a woman allows the warmth of herbal steam to permeate the vagina to cleanse and revitalize the uterus. Although this process most commonly reduces discomfort associated with menstruation, there are many more benefits. Vaginal Steams use a combination of specially formulated herbal blends dependent on each individual's needs. Each session also includes complimentary water to stay hydrated. Vaginal steaming has been documented to have many benefits for a woman's overall reproductive health. Women suffering from

cysts, fibroids, endometriosis, Human Papilloma Virus (HPV), bacteria infections, yeast infections, heavy menses, or painful cramps have gotten positive outcomes from steaming. Furthermore, a post-partum cleansing of the womb is essential after delivery to prevent infections, uterine prolapse, or other adverse outcomes. Steaming monthly can also be used as a preventative method to getting infections. Most women steam one to two times per month and others once every six weeks, depending on each client's needs. Buy your steamer for home use https://amzn. to/3Pb5K8V

5. Salt baths are great for regulating the vaginal ph and restoring moisture because water chases salt. Salt baths relieves inflammation and muscle soreness. If the sitz bath is for a vaginal infection, adding ½ cup of table vinegar with the salt can be helpful. Add coconut oil to restore moisture and to add a sweet fragrance.

6. Eat fiber to help you have regular bowel movements. I say at least 3 to 5 bowel movements per day is healthy. Constipation and pelvic floor problems often go hand in hand. Often symptoms such as pelvic pain, painful intercourse, urge incontinence and prolapse exist alongside constipation. You can see how extra stool in the bowel can put increased pressure on the rest of the pelvic organs. There are a lot of reason you may become constipated. Thankfully, most can be fixed with a change in diet or tweak in medication. For some women, though, their inability to get it all out may be due to a rectocele. A rectocele is a bulging of the rectum into the vagina. It happens when the wall between the rectum and vagina becomes weak, and the rectum starts to press internally against the wall. This can cause serious constipation and discomfort, as the rectum balloons out and creates a kink in your stool's normal path out the body. If it gets big enough, it can push its way out of the vaginal opening, Kyle G. Cologne, M.D., assistant professor of colorectal surgery at the Keck School of Medicine at USC and member of The American Society of Colon and Rectal Surgeons (ASCRS)

7. Insert one phd boric acid capsule in your vagina to regulate your ph. Insert one right before sex to prevent ph imbalance caused by sex. This treats bad odor causing bacteria and yeast overgrowth in the vagina. I use them before and after sex for the best results. Please take as directed

on the bottle.

8. Wipe front to back holding the labia open and drop the wipe or tissue, then repeat until clean. It is best to use balanced wipes for cleaning after using the bathroom. If you are home, a shower would be ideal. Never use alcohol wipes. They expand the vagina and throw in the vaginal ph

9. Eat fruit three times per day. Apples may help keep the vagina lubricated, probiotic-rich foods may help regulate the microorganisms in your vagina, and high-fiber foods may help prevent BV. Kiwi fruit contains a high level of vitamin C and antioxidants that help to boost the good bacteria in the vagina to help keep it healthy and well lubricated. Avocados serve as a good natural remedy for skin darkening, roughness and facial pimples. The substance helps to keep the skin glowing, soft and fresh. Notwithstanding the skin treatment it provides, the large consumption of avocados helps to prevent vaginal dryness. Orange is one of the most popular fruits nationwide. It is filled with vitamin C, which is known to have various health benefits. This includes; preventing skin damage, lowering cholesterol, controlling blood sugar levels, and keeping the vagina lubricated, among other benefits. Fruit provides vital reproductive nutrients.

Many fruits are also high in antioxidants, which are great for improving blood flow, keeping your cells healthy,reducing oxidative stress— which plays a role in fertility.

Fruits high in antioxidants include:

- Pomegranates

- Blueberries

- Raspberries

- Strawberries

- Apples

- Goji berries

1. Bonus: Women who consume more citrus fruit are less likely to develop uterine fibroids. Also women who get along with other women. Women who have issues with other women bodies turn on itself because the body obeys in hating women so since you are a woman it turns on you.

5. The high level of vitamin C in orange helps to stimulate wetness of the vaginal walls to help penetration during sexual intercourse easier. It provides the body with stamina, which means it can aid in lasting long during sexual intercourse. It keeps the sex drive going well, by eradicating the free radicals that slows down the normal energy level as regards sexual health.

6. Tify the effects of acidity. Citrus fruits are slightly acidic while most fruits — like oranges, tangerines, and kiwis — are good sources of vitamin C, which helps build collagen and protects cells from free-radical damage.One orange provides 116.2 percent of the daily value of vitamin C, making it a great way to keep your body and sexual drive healthy. Avocados are also filled with vitamin E, which is a major antioxidant that helps regulate blood flow to the vitamin C content in orange is at a high rate than any other citrus fruits. One orange provides 116.2 percent of the daily value of Vitamin C. So, one orange a day can help to keep your body system and sexual drive healthy. Cranberry juice helps tackle UTIs Cranberry juice (100% cranberry juice — not the sweetened stuff) or concentrated extract capsules are full of antioxidants and acidic compounds, which are powerful infection fighters that can help bacteria from adhering to the bladder wall. Studies how Trusted Source that 100 percent cranberry products can be especially beneficial in preventing UTIs in women with recurrent or recent UTI issues. Just make sure you stay away from the sugar-loaded cranberry juice varieties, which can actually make things worse down there. Oranges can be consumed in their raw form or juiced, depending on how you enjoy it the most. Vaginal dryness can lead to bruising of the vaginal walls, which can cause minimal bleeding and pain during sex or after sex. When the vagina experiences are such, it can be highly uncomfortable and decrease orgasm which according to scientific studies, helps to release hormones that can provide relief from

stress, improve moods, and boost immunity. It is recommended to make fruits part of your daily consumption to stay healthy.

Avocados are also filled with Vitamin E which is a major antioxidant that helps regulate the blood flow to the vagina. It is also rich in potassium and vitamin B6 which certain studies show can decrease premenstrual syndrome symptoms like; irritability, bloating and fatigue. This can help to boost a woman's libido and energy during sexual intercourse. Avocados contains the vitamin B6, which some studies show can decrease symptoms of premenstrual syndrome (such as fatigue, bloating, and irritability). This might make it easier for women to "get in the mood." For men, avocado can also increase libido a little more indirectly.

Soy helps improve vaginal dryness.

Soy can be a bit of a controversial topic. But the phytoestrogens—compounds that mimic estrogen in the body — found in soy are good news for vaginal health, especially in people with reduced estrogen levels. There are many reasons for decreased estrogen levels in the body, from medications to menopause. But one of the major symptoms of low estrogen is vaginal dryness.

So, here's how soy helps: Minimally-processed soy products are hydrophilic (which allows your muscles to retain more water) and contain isoflavones (a plant-derived phytoestrogen) that are beneficial for the skin in postmenopausal women.

Research shows

Trusted Source that soy dietary supplements can help improve vaginal dryness in post menopausal women when compared to a placebo. It's important to note that most studies focus on supplements with high levels of isoflavones, which may not be present in all foods.

8 .Wear cotton underwear to allow oxygen to flow and keep the vagina cool

9. Never wear nylon panties they hold moisture and is an incubator for bacteria to grow causing foul order, itching, painful sex, and raw skin

10. Use period panties or organic chemical free sanitary napkins. Only wear tampons when really necessary and change them every two hours.

11. Drink Kombucha 8 hours before sex and immediately after sex.

12. Never walk around in wet swim suits change them immediately after swimming.

13. The naturally neutral pH is equal to 7, but the normal vaginal pH ranges between 3.8 and 5.0, which is moderately acidic [2]. A lower pH value (more acidic) in the vagina than the blood or interstitial fluids can protect vaginal mucosa from pathogenic organisms [4].Most fruits and vegetables tend to be base food items, which means they're above 7 on the pH scale, according to the International Food Information Council Foundation. Plant-based proteins fall into this category too.

14. Apple Juice cleanses the digestive tract. Apples are a natural source of pectin, a soluble fiber that moves food through your digestive system and keeps you regular. Bonus benefit: Your good gut bacteria love to feed on pectin. Some experts think that pectin helps the good bacteria multiply, which may help ward off some chronic diseases and cancer in the gut.

15. Colonics cleanse all the backed up waste out of your intestines so you don't smell like crap. A colonic involves using large amounts of water to flush waste out of the colon, the longest part of the large intestine. The procedure is also known as colonic irrigation, colon hydrotherapy, or a colon cleanse.

16. Detox teas cleanse the digestive system where most illness and odors begin. Click the link to get your detox tea today. https://shop. totallifechanges.com/instt-en-b2-zz/instt-en-b2-zzhtml?lang=en&ccode

=us&sponsor=Acooley Do not over use tea because it can cause kidney failure. You want to gently detox for a few days then allow the body to rest and rejuvenate.

18. Sleep take naps to rejuvenate the whole body. If you are well rested sex will be better and all the organs including your brain will function better. The brain plays a huge part in how your body responds and feels. Make sure you get a full 6 to 8 hours of restful sleep at night. A great way is to have great sex that tires you out. By reading this book I am sure you will be well rested at night.

19. Olive oil Keeps your body lubricated. There nothing like a juicy peach Olive oil is likely safe and effective to use as a lube when penetration isn't involved. Benefits of Olive Oil

Olive oil has many different health benefits, including:

• Cardiovascular health: Extra virgin olive oil contains two types of healthy fats, mono saturated fats and polyunsaturated fat, both of which help reduce bad cholesterol levels and, in turn, lower the risk of heart disease and strokes.

• Digestive health: Olive oil lubricates the intestinal tract and may also help reduce the production of gastric acid.

• Inflammation relief: Extra virgin olive oil contains oleocanthal, an antioxidant with significant anti-inflammatory properties.

• Blood sugar stabilization: Olive oil can help reduce glycemic response to high-glycemic foods, which, in turn, can help manage Type 1 and Type 2 diabetes.

• Healthy skin and hair: Extra virgin olive oil is high in both vitamin E and vitamin K, both of which are essential for maintaining healthy skin and hair.

• Constipation relief: Consuming olive oil may help soften stool and relieve constipation.

20. Kimichi smells horrible so eat it outside and when you are separated from your significant other until it does its job of regulating the bad bacteria.

21. Cantaloupe aids in proper hydration can help with your vagina's self lubrication and reduces non hereditary or illness caused gray hair down there

22. Pickles are full of vitamin K to keep the peach pretty. Vitamin K plays a role in skin health primarily through its involvement in blood clotting and wound healing.

Here's how it helps the skin:

Wound Healing: Vitamin K is essential for the production of proteins that help in blood clotting, including clotting factors II, VII, IX, and X. When you have a wound, these clotting factors work together to stop bleeding by forming a clot. This prevents excessive blood loss and provides a controlled environment for the wound to heal.

Reducing Bruising: Vitamin K can help reduce the appearance of bruises, especially those caused by minor injuries or surgeries. It does this by assisting in the breakdown of heme, a component of hemoglobin that gives blood its red color. This breakdown helps clear the area of blood that has leaked from damaged blood vessels.

Skin Elasticity: Some research suggests that vitamin K may contribute to skin elasticity and the reduction of wrinkles. It is thought to do this by promoting the production of collagen, a protein that helps maintain skin's firmness and structure.

While vitamin K is important for skin health, it's worth noting that a balanced diet typically provides an adequate amount of this vitamin for most people. Severe vitamin K deficiency is rare and usually only occurs in specific medical conditions or as a result of certain medications. If you're concerned about your skin health or bruising, it's best to consult a healthcare professional for a proper evaluation and advice.

ifies the risk of blindly transmitting an infection to any new partner in a monogamous relationship.

23. Green leafy vegetables and sweet potatoes have many beneficial properties - even for your vaginal health. Rich in beta carotene and Vitamin A, sweet potatoes help maintain healthy mucous membranes, which means they may help prevent bacterial vaginosis (BV), a common vaginal infection. Vitamin A deficiency, along with deficiencies in vitamins C, D, E, calcium, folate, and beta Green leafy vegetables and sweet Potatoes have some sweet benefits, even for your vaginal health. Rich in beta carotene and vitamin A, sweet potatoes help keep your mucous membranes healthy. This means they can help prevent bacterial vaginosis (BV), a common vaginal infection. Vitamin A deficiency, along with deficiencies in vitamins C, D, E, calcium, folate, and beta-carotene, associated with increased bv. So, eat up!

Sweet potatoes are also high in fiber, which may help stabilize insulin levels

Trusted Source

24. In those Polycystic Ovarian Syndrome (POS) . Insulin resistance is common with PCOS — so by regulating blood sugar over the course of several months, the fiber in sweet potatoes may promote fertility and help to reduce symptoms.

25. Wax all the hair off the peach no peach fuzz needed. Hair holds sweat and odors. Plus a bald peach looks better. This is not 1970 where you need an afro in your pants. Do not use razors because you can get razor burn, razor bumps, swelling, hyperpigmentation and irritation. I learned this the hard way one day I had to sleep with an ice pack between my legs after using razors.

26. Avoid leather and plastic apparel in warm environments that's like baking the peach. We aren't making peach cobbler so maintain proper body temperature for fresh smells. These materials can trap heat and moisture, leading to undesirable odors and skin irritations. Opting for breathable fabrics like cotton or linen, along with adequate ventilation, can help keep you feeling cool, comfortable, and smelling fresh, even in the heat of summer.

27. Get your peach checked before and after new partners, because your health and well-being should always be a top priority. In this chapter, we emphasize the importance of regular health check-ups and making informed decisions in intimate relationships. While the ideal scenario is finding a God-aligned and chosen life partner, it's crucial to be prepared for the complexities of modern dating and relationships.

Before diving into any new relationship, consider taking the time to understand your own physical and emotional health. Regular check-ups with healthcare professionals ensure that you're in optimal condition. It's not just about physical health; emotional well-being is equally important. Reflect on your boundaries, values, and what you desire in a partner.

After entering a new relationship, continue to prioritize self-care and open communication. Regular check-ins with yourself and your partner can help maintain a healthy and harmonious connection. Remember, it's not just about praying for the ideal partner but also actively participating in building a nurturing and respectful relationship.

Ultimately, thi tip is to encourage you to be proactive about your health and emotional well-being while pursuing a loving and fulfilling partnership that aligns with your beliefs and values.

Prioritizing Safe and Responsible Choices.

28. Use protection when having sexual relationships with anyone that isn't long-term or with whom you have no commitment. In this chapter, we delve into the crucial importance of sexual health and responsible decision-making when it comes to intimate encounters.

Protecting yourself and your partner(s) is not just a matter of physical well-being; it's also about respecting one another and fostering open communication. While long-term committed relationships often involve trust and mutual agreements, in other situations, using protection is a fundamental step in safeguarding your health and that of your partner.

Remember, the decision to use protection is a responsible and caring choice that ensures your physical health and emotional well-being remain a top priority. It's a sign of maturity and respect for both yourself and your partner(s), allowing for safer and more enjoyable intimate experiences while reducing the risk of unwanted consequences.

29. Get tested for STIs with your partner STI testing offers peace of mind because it's the only way to confirm whether you have an STI, which could develop into a more serious condition. STI testing also:

• Protects your partner's health and helps stop the spread or development of STIs

• Helps you get early and effective treatment

• Helps protect your fertility, since untreated STIs can lead to infertility

• Protects your unborn baby from infection

30. Choose who experiences the peach wisely The wrong men can damage your peach, but the right man can help heal your peach.

Masturbating is repelling partners because you are saying you do not need a mate. Abusing your vagina with multiple and random partners is causing spiritual wars inside of you. The deposits of each man's spirit is at war with one another. The body can regenerate and heal when you eat well, detox spiritually and physically, and rest. Tips to know he is the right man first you know who God is and his character because a man that spends time with God will be like him. Second know who you are completely. If you are a world traveler then you know you aren't a truck driver or farmer's wife. If you like luxury them you can't be with a hobo sexual. The quality of woman you are is the quality of man you will attract. Listen to what a man says and watch his actions see if they align. Ask God he promised to Give you wisdom holding nothing back. What ever you say and think is what you will create and get. Only speak what you desire and never pay attention to anything opposite of that. Mother's hug your daughters and sons so the can thrive and heal. Talk to them about this book.

Prayer Lord I repent for allowing every filthy, abusive, disgusting spirit, and man in my womb that wasn't my God ordained husband. Lord cleanse and purify my womb restore and make it brand new. If you are a man reading it pray it for your wife and pray that your penis is cleansed from every filthy, unclean spirit, and woman that my penis has entered. May all unGodly soul ties be severed and destroyed that they may not enter into my God ordained marriage. This marriage bed is holy sanctified and undefiled. 34. Don't allow men with bad oral hygiene eat the peach. You don't want his gingivitis causing bacteria in your peach smelling up the peach. Remedy for bad breath and digestion issues eat cardamom, ground clove, cinnamon, and mint leaves.

31. Prioritizing Hygiene and Health in Intimate Moments

32. Make sure your partner bathes with pH-friendly soaps before sex. In this chapter, we explore the significance of personal hygiene in intimate relationships and how it can contribute to a more comfortable and enjoyable experience for both partners.

Maintaining good personal hygiene is a sign of respect for yourself and your partner. Using pH-balanced soaps before engaging in sexual activities helps ensure a clean and pleasant encounter. Proper hygiene can also reduce the risk of irritations, infections, or discomfort that may arise from intimate contact.

This chapter offers practical advice on discussing personal hygiene with your partner in a respectful and sensitive manner. Effective communication about such matters is essential to ensure both individuals feel comfortable and cared for in the relationship.

Additionally, it emphasizes the importance of mutual responsibility, with both partners taking steps to maintain hygiene and health. By doing so, you can enhance the physical and emotional connection between you and your partner, creating a more positive and enjoyable intimate bond.

Make sure your partner eats a clean healthy diet so he isn't passing bad bacteria, parasites, and viruses to you

Wash sex toys with PH balances soaps and water Dietary Choices: A clean, healthy diet not only benefits overall health but also plays a role in sexual well-being. Encouraging your partner to maintain a balanced diet can reduce the risk of transmitting harmful bacteria, parasites, or viruses during intimate moments. By consuming nutritious foods, you promote good gut health and bolster the immune system, which can help prevent potential health concerns. This chapter offers guidance on approaching discussions about dietary choices with sensitivity and care, emphasizing the mutual responsibility for each other's health.

Sex Toy Hygiene: Properly cleaning sex toys with pH-balanced soaps and water is essential to prevent infections and maintain personal hygiene. This chapter provides practical advice on the correct methods for cleaning and storing sex toys, emphasizing the importance of regular maintenance. It also touches on the importance of mutual consent and communication when incorporating sex toys into your intimate moments, ensuring a safe and enjoyable experience for both partners.

33. Wear appropriate size underwear to prevent chafing and irritation.

34. Never use baby powder (causes ovarian cancer) or heavy perfumes they interfere with the PH and good bacteria, and cause

35. Work your muscles by doing Kegels set the alarm in your phone to do them every hour

36. Have sex to tighten your muscles have your partner coach your muscles back in shape

37. Have orgasms during sex. An orgasm is the height or peak of sexual arousal when the body releases sexual tension and pressure. It involves very intense feelings of pleasure in your genitals and throughout your body. An orgasm usually lasts a few seconds and feels very good. Orgasm occurs during sexual stimulation of your genitals and sexual (erogenous) zones of your body. These include the:

- Penis.

- Testicles.

- Clitoris.

- Vagina.

- Nipples.

- Anus.

It is one of four stages in the body's sexual response cycle

1. Desire (libido).

2. Excitement (arousal).

3. Orgasm.

4. Resolution. Benefits of Orgasm For Your Health

Female pleasure is something you always deserve, period. Now that we know orgasms release feel-good neurochemicals like dopamine and oxytocin, we wanted to name some of the other incredible benefits of the female orgasm. To start, did you know that the female orgasm boosts your satisfaction and activates the reward circuits in your brain, turning on the part of your mind that makes you feel euphoric? Here are some more benefits of giving yourself some solo self-care time.

1. Clearer skin: This benefit also has to do with your oxytocin levels. Many studies have shown that low levels of oxytocin in the bloodstream are correlated with high levels of stress, tension, and anxiety.

2. Glowing skin: According to Healthline, a post-sex glow (yes, solo sex is still sex) is a real thing. When you're engaging in sexual activity, there's an increase in the rate of blood flowing through your body, meaning more of those blood cells carrying oxygen can reach your face.

3. Less stress: When you orgasm, your entire body focuses on achieving this feat. In turn, you quiet your mind as well. In addition to all we've mentioned above, there's so much less anxiety and mental struggle your body endures if you take the time to orgasm.

4. Falling asleep faster: Achieving orgasm is a workout! It can tire your body out, thus allowing you to fall asleep faster. While quieting your mind and exhausting your body, masturbation can help you hit the hay as soon as you're ready to.

5. Increasing your libido: According to MedicalNewsToday, there may be an association between masturbating and a person's sex drive.

Their research suggests that married women who masturbate may have a higher sex drive than those who do not. It makes sense to us!

6. Burning those calories: Get that workout in, girl! According to Time, sex demanded 101 calories from men and just 69 from women, burning an average of 3.6 calories per minute

7. Counteracting menopause: Wait, what?! Yes, you heard us correctly. According to the Mayo Clinic, masturbating increases blood flow to the vagina, which may help counteract menopause's uncomfortable effects on the area.

8. Relieving menstrual cramps: It's a natural pain reliever! According to Healthline, "masturbating can help relieve anything from cramps and back pain to headaches and joint aches," says Ross. That's because, during orgasm, the body releases a rush of dopamine and serotonin."

9. Strengthening your immune system: 1. In a study conducted by the National Library of Medicine, it was found that sexual arousal and orgasms activated components of the immune system.

38. Be honest about sex make sure you are enjoying it. Be honest about who you are, what you like, your boundaries, your desires, and make sure before sex you are compatible with the person you intend to have sex with. Ask your partner what he likes and dislikes. (I pray your partner is your God ordained husband)

39. Urinate after sex Urinating after sex may help to flush bacteria out of the urethra, thereby helping to prevent a urinary tract infection (UTI). It may be especially helpful for women, or people who are prone to UTIs. However, peeing after sex will not prevent pregnancy or sexually transmitted infections (STIs).

40. Take care of your mental health so the rest of you can be whole. Have fun with friends, see a therapist if needed. Reduce your stress by delegating tasks. Organize your life. Sleep in a clean environment.

41. Moisturize the outer skin at night and sleep naked to get more oxygen to the peach

42. Brush your teeth, Brush your tongue, and floss regularly to prevent bad bacteria from transferring orally and to your peach and his penis.

43. Speak these affirmations over your peach

1. My peach is powerful.

2. My peach is juicy

3. My peach is pleasurable

4. My husband is in love with my peach while looking at his picture

5. My peach is tight while doing kegels

6. My Peach is healthy while eating healthy

7. My Peach tastes delicious while receiving oral sex

8. My Peach smells delicious while bathing

9. My Peach is youthful while bathing

10. My peach is is fertile before and during sex

11. My Peach is Pretty while getting undressed

12. Meditate and heal your peach throughout the day

44. Avoid eating too much sugar, candy, and salt. Use honey as a sweetener. Avoid chemical sweeteners because they cause bacteria to overgrow and cause fowl odors.

45. Avoid coffee it is a dierctic that causes dehydration and no one likes a dry peach. Also avoid carbonated drinks that cause gas and bloating before sex. You don't want to run him away. On dates drink still wine and still water afterwards.

46. Never allow a man to go from anal to vaginal with out proper cleaning in between. Bad bacteria is in the waste found in your anus and should not be in your vagina. Simplifi ed don't put crap in your vagina.

47. Drink 64 to 72 ounces of water per day to stay hydrated. The endocervical canal is lined with a moist mucous membrane. Cells within this tissue layer secrete fluids and project minute hairlike structures called cilia that help to move sperm through the canal. The fluids given off consist mainly of water, sugars, starches, and proteins. During ovulation (when the ovaries release an egg) the mucous secretions are plentiful and watery; before and after ovulation the secretions are thick and relatively scant. Th e mucus is arranged in a meshlike pattern of filaments and spaces. During ovulation, the openings in the meshwork of fi laments become larger so that sperm may freely pass through. Lysozyme also present in cervical mucus, is an enzyme that helps to destroy certain types of bacteria and acts as a defense against infections.

48. Have your man suck your breast to help tighten the vagina it works the same as a baby sucking the milk out your breast. Th e stimulation of women's nipples from suckling, including breastfeeding, promotes the production and release of oxytocin and prolactin.

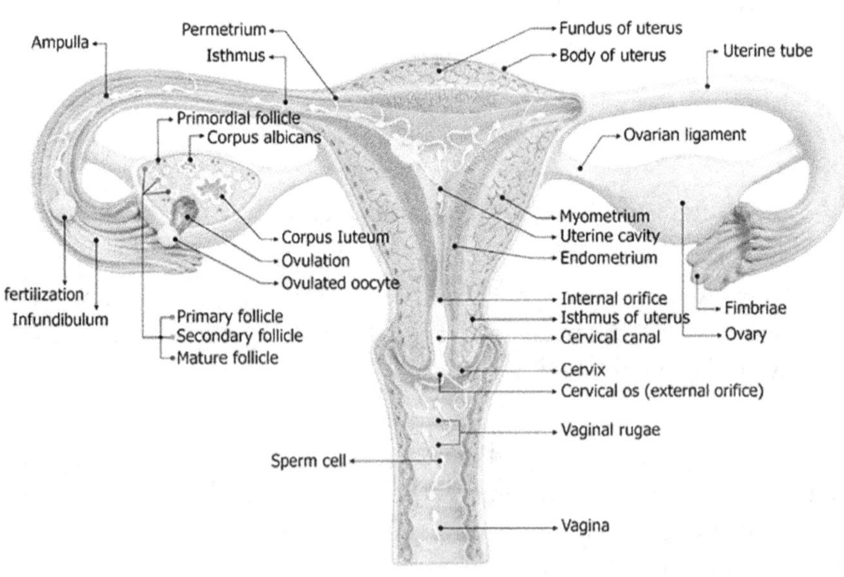

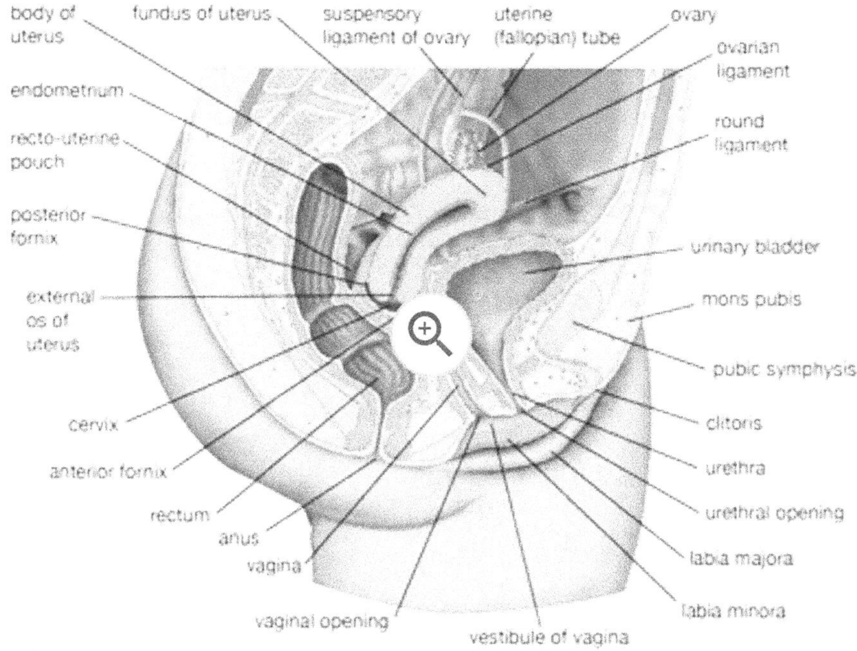

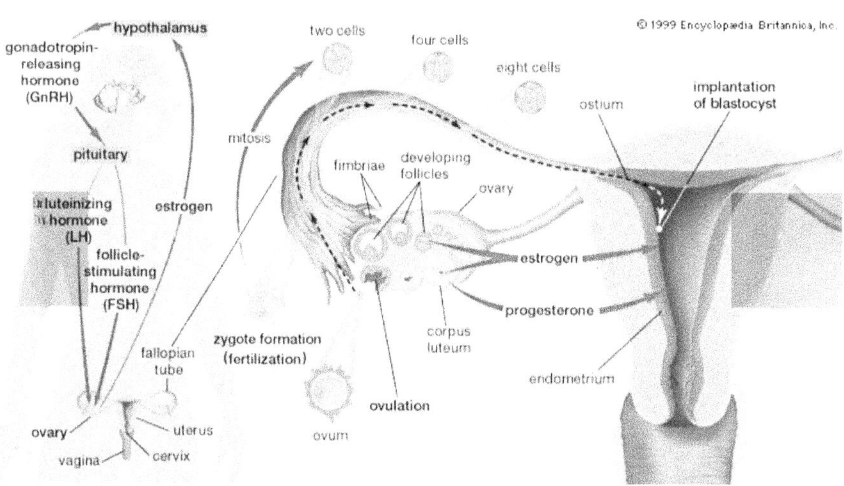

49. The hypothalamus and pituitary gland control the secretion of gonadotropins (luteinizing hormone and follicle-stimulating hormone) that regulate the processes of ovulation and menstruation in women. Gonadotropin-releasing hormone is secreted from the

hypothalamus in response to neuronal activity in the limbic region of the brain, which is predominantly influenced by emotional and sexual factors. Gonadotropinreleasing hormone stimulates the secretion of gonadotropins from the pituitary gland that then stimulate cells in the ovary to synthesize and secrete estrogen and progesterone. Increased serum concentrations of estrogen and progesterone provide negative feedback signaling in the hypothalamus to inhibit further secretion of gonadotropin-releasing hormone.

50. Foods that can naturally increase estrogen are those you'd find in a plant-based diet. You can also consider vitamins and minerals to boost estrogen. For example, consider soy products and those with phytoestrogens, such as the ones below.

- Legumes – lentils

- Garlic oil (do not over do because you will stink so balance it with fruit)

- Nuts and seeds

- Flaxseeds and sesame seeds

- Soy-miso and tofu

- Fruits – dried fruits and oranges, strawberries and peaches

- Vegetables – kale, sprouts, celery

• Yohimbe is an evergreen tree native to central and western Africa. It has a compound called yohimbine in its bark. The bark has been used traditionally as an aphrodisiac and to enhance sexual performance.

51. The bones of the pelvis are a critical part of the central portion of the skeleton. They serve as a transition from the axial skeleton and the appendicular skeleton of the lower body, serving as an attachment point for some of the strongest muscles in the human body while withstanding the forces generated by them. Maintain a healthy weight. Avoid becoming constipated. Lift with care. Exercise your pelvic floor muscles and your core. Learn to relax your pelvic floor. Practice good posture. Protect your pelvic floor when you work out – modify exercises if you have a pelvic floor issue. Kegels improve blood circulation to the pelvic floor and vagina, and this may be helpful for arousal and lubrication. Do core exercises like aerial arts, pole dance, etc. Reasons Women are Drawn to

• Vaginal Strengthening Exercises

• During pregnancy for an easier labor and delivery

• After vaginal childbirth to help resolve the pelvic trauma and damage

• As the vagina loses some of its natural elasticity with age

• To improve sexual experience

• To prevent pelvic organ prolapse

Whatever your reason, incorporating pelvic floor exercises into your routine will strengthen and tone these important muscles. It may also make it easier to for you to achieve orgasm and kick-up orgasm intensity.

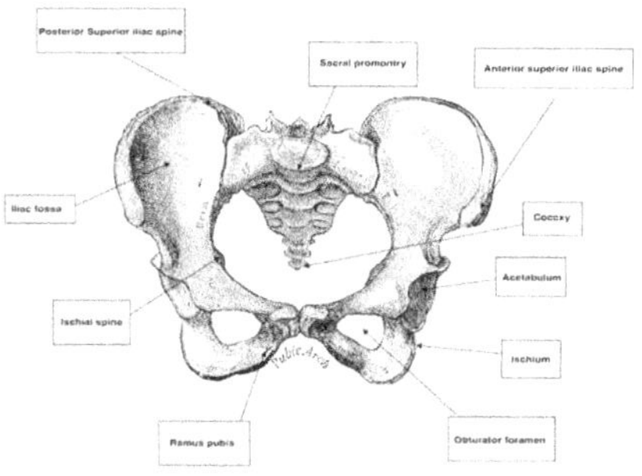

52. Stop traumatizing your uterus Tampons are invasive products your uterus was designed to hold a tampon. Tampons can cause Toxic Shock Syndrome. The body goes into shock because there is a foreign object sticking in it like a stopper in a tub. The blood needs to flow out like water in a tub when you take the stopper out. Tampons help bad bacteria grow in the vagina and can cause abrasions that harbor bad bateria. I suggest wearing period panties. They look like regular underwear, but they're designed to keep moisture away from your skin as they soak up menstrual blood. The fabric in period underwear contains a moisturewicking fabric made up of thousands of small filaments. These fibers trap blood or other liquid to keep it from leaking onto your clothes.

53. Pap smears are harmful and helpful Paps smears involve winding up and open the cervix which isn't normal for the body and scrapping of the cells which is causing abrasions that can lead to bacteria infections. If done improperly can cause prolapse. Doctors often hide the risks because their reward in pay is of greater importance to them. A Pap test helps find cervical cancer early before you have symptoms. A Pap test helps find cervical cancer and some STIs before it spreads when it is easier to treat. Choose your Obgyn carefully and speak up if you feel too much pulling, pressure, or discomfort. Be your own advocate. This is your body.

54. Forgive and love other women as if they were yourself because hate for other women manifests illness in your body because your body turns against itself because you are a woman. You reap what you sow. James 3:17-18 (New International Version) Share Audio But the wisdom that comes from heaven is first of all pure; then peace-loving, considerate, submissive, full of mercy and good fruit, impartial and sincere. Peacemakers who sow in peace reap a harvest of righteousness. I pray all seeds of perversion are removed from your mind and womb. May your peach bring forth Good fruit and only good seed come from your peach. The laws God gave us to govern our bodies is so we live long happy lives that represent him in the world.

55. Ginseng

Experiments indicate ginseng improves the libido in both males and females. And some small studies have shown it may be helpful for erectile dysfunction.

56. Oysters

Commonly claimed as the ultimate natural libido booster, oysters contain zinc which helps raise testosterone levels. But you'd need to eat around 50 to have an impact on your sexual desire – making it a very expensive option.

57. Truffles

Truffles have an aroma similar to aldosterone – a male pheromone that boosts female arousal levels. We ladies are simple creatures. Treat us to truffles and our libidos will be sky-high.

58. Ginger

The aroma stimulates the arousal centre in the brain. Ginger is also available in the form of bath salts. I have tried this and it makes the blood rush to the labial and clitoral areas, making you so horny that you will want to rush to the bedroom!

It also works for men by stimulating blood flow in the testicular area.

59. To heal external scars use tea tree oil oil, honey, helichrysum oil, Calendula oil , frankincense oil, emu oil, vetiver oil, aloe vera drink and on skin, shea butter, coconut oil, vitamin c oil, onion, banana peel, olive oil, apple cider vinegar, milk in bath, and yogurt on skin

To heal internal scars. Massage helps to break up scar tissue/adhesion formation.

1. Helps the uterus to rid itself of old stagnant blood and tissues.

2. Brings fresh oxygenated blood to the uterus.

3. Helps to strengthen the uterine muscles.

4. Reduces inflammation.

5. Helps the body to loosen tight or twisted tissues.

• A rectovaginal fistula is a connection that should not exist between the lower part of the large intestine — the rectum or anus — and the vagina. Bowel contents can leak through the fistula, allowing gas or stool to pass through the vagina.

• Crohn's disease or other inflammatory bowel disease.

• Radiation treatment or cancer in the pelvic area.

• Complication after surgery in the pelvic area.

• Complication from diverticulitis, an infection of small, bulging pouches in the digestive tract.

• Injury during childbirth.

Best Home Remedies for Anal Fistula:

• Sitz bath Sitz bath is one of the best ways to aid symptoms of anal fistula that include irritation, swelling, pain, and inflammation. A sitz bath is a process of soaking the anal area in plain warm water. The water should not be very hot. A fistula patient should take sitz baths at least 3-4 times every day. (Also Read: How to take a sitz bath and its benefits)

• Eat healthy Take care of your diet and keep your stomach and digestive system healthy. Avoid spicy food, junk food, and fatty food and improve digestive conditions that are less prone to problems. Choose more whole grains, leafy green vegetables, fruits, and lean meats. Adding fibers and cereal to your diet will help to avoid constipation, which can irritate a fistula. Some kitchen hacks that you can use to aid symptoms of fistula are:

• Honey: Honey is an antimicrobial component and its daily

consumption is good for overall health. Take one tablespoon of honey and mix it in a glass of lukewarm water.

• Coconut oil: You can apply coconut oil to the anal sphincter and you can also include it in your diet.

• Oregano Oil: You can use oregano oil for fistula treatment. The oil has antibacterial, antiviral, antibiotic, and anti-inflammatory properties.

• Flax Seeds: Take a glass of water and add one tablespoon of flaxseed powder. Stir it well and have it before going to bed. It helps in controlling bowel movements.

Drink water Drink plenty of water; it will act as one of the best home remedies for fistula. Avoid alcohol and soda; as a substitute consume huge amounts of water and fruit juices. You can have ginger tea, turmeric milk, etc. This will prevent constipation, which gives pressure on your fistula. An excess amount of water will make waste softer and will help clean the intestines.

Use donut pillows If your job needs you to sit down for long hours, avoid the extra pressure on your back, buttocks, and legs, particularly, if you have an anal fistula. This could be done by sitting on a "donut pillow" instead of the regular chair or on the toilet seat directly. Donut pillows are one of the best home remedies for piles.

60. Maintain good toilet hygiene Always wash your anal area after each bowel movement or going to the toilet. Avoid any bacteria residual on your skin, as, it is the first step to prevent an infection. If you're outside and can't wash, always keep wipes with you to be used until you can get home. Your hands get the most exposure to germs and therefore you must clean them regularly. Change your underclothing as needed throughout the day if the fistula is leaking. This will prevent the spread of germs and growth of bacteria which can decrease the peri-anal irritation and thus, it help in removing the annoying symptoms associated with fistulas.

Improve your immune system Having a healthy diet and eating food, like fish, olive oil, and citrus fruits which are rich in omega-3s, omega-6s, and vitamin C will help you to strengthen the immune system and decrease the levels of inflammation you may suffer due to a fistula.

61. Majority of what happens to the body starts in the mind and spirit. Make sure you think you are healthy and worth being loved.

62. Lake of Intimacy causes a great deal of vaginal and reproductive issues because love is a need. We were created to have sex with our husbands not random men that damage you spiritually, emotionally, physically, and cellularly.

63. Forgive yourself and others so that you are whole inwardly and outwardly.

64. Your body is a refelection of what you think and feel about yourself. Love you and do things that pamper you like going to the spa, watching funny movies, loving others for no reason.

65. Use Aroma therapy and relaxing melodic music to create a pleasant serene atmosphere for yourself.

66. Get out and meet other women that are leading healthy lifestyles. Socialization is a need.

67. Stop eating greasy garbage food and treat your body like God lives in it. Treat it like a beautiful temple. Dress up in beautiful clothes and spray beautiful fragrances on your clothes not your peach. Here are some great scents that attract men click the link now https://www.marykay.com/msameca/en-us/products/all/bella-belara-eau-de-parfum-150206 https://www.marykay.com/msameca/en-us/products/all/cityscape-eaude-parfum-150225

68. Stop speaking negatively about men because you will manifest that in your life. Speak only what you desire in your life.

Click the link to:

https://tap.bio/@Amecatravelinit?fbclid=PAAaZvs7nJZ-
2VEkvL-nBmafQ5lCOfQ3T6yeZixcIgxck54oB9WhMAlrTt8sqaQ_
aem_AVnVjAGzZsD8FUyBcH55aMuHWPugtfPllZGHzQqu5mH_
CFx_GT1OUSRpdd8jmuByK88

69. Powerful Pleasant Peach shopping list

https://tap.bio/@Amecatravelinit?fbclid=PAAabg1VWG2pm0jkqt-
G0dNI8SvRpCo20HDmlsUlH5S7bs9qI5akLqOi809nJk_aem_ AWn-
q5h_Q-
My favorite the peach for the peach https://amzn.to/3P9GgZf

Yohimbe
https://amzn.to/3Rc8Vjk

Manuka oil
https://amzn.to/486Gk4Uhelichrysumoil https://amzn.to/3EtrVSF
vetiver oil
https://amzn.to/45HeAC7 Vitamin c https://amzn.to/3Rc2893

Calendula oil
https://amzn.to/3Errw34

Frankincense
https://amzn.to/3LfrTBz soy miso
https://amzn.to/3sL0cdF

Flaxseed
https://amzn.to/3Z7kFoW

Vsteam
https://amzn.to/3Pb5K8V Virgin Coconut Oil https://amzn.to/3PsqI-
jN Hyaluronic Acid and Vitamin C https://amzn.to/3L8yRZi Collagen Supplements https://amzn.to/44H5vrG

Boric Acid Vaginal Suppositories for Vaginal Odor by pH-D Feminine Health, #1 Doctor Recommended, Woman Owned, 36ct,

Made in https://amzn.to/44C942s

Amazon Basics Epsom Salt Soaking Aid, Lavender Scented, 3 Pound, https://amzn.to/485SN8P

Amazon Basics Epsom Salt Soaking Aid, Lavender Scented, 3

Pound,
https://amzn.to/3Evddui Liquid I.V. Hydration Multiplier + Probiotic Kombucha - Tart

Green Apple - Hydration Powder Packets | Electrolyte Drink Mix | Easy Open Single-Serving Stick | Non-GMO | 14 Sticks
https://amzn.to/3RbD9ml

Health-Ade Organic Passion Tangerine Kombucha, https://amzn.to/3sIMc45
https://livewellplants.etsy.com

Remember to read all ingredients to prevent allergic reactions, consult a physician if symptoms increase, and test skin products on the hand first

To find out causes of specific diseases and natural treatments read my book Title: "Metaphysical Insights into Health and Wellness: Unveiling the Spiritual Connection"

To my husband I am so glad my body belongs only to you and God.

May my peach always bring you pleasure.

Certainly, here's a chapter that explores soul ties and sexual sin with the aid of Bible scriptures:

Untangling the Complexity of Soul Ties and Sexual Sin

Opening Scripture: 1 Corinthians 6:18 (NIV) - "Flee from sexual immorality. All other sins a person commits are outside the body, but whoever sins sexually, sins against their own body."

Sexual sin has repercussions that extend beyond the physical act, reaching into the realm of the emotional, mental, and spiritual. This chapter aims to explore the concept of soul ties and the implications of sexual sin, drawing insights from Biblical wisdom.

Understanding Soul Ties

The Bible doesn't explicitly mention "soul ties," but it does emphasize the deep connection established through sexual intimacy. Scripture teaches that sexual relations create a profound bond between two individuals, intertwining their spirits and souls. This bond goes beyond the physical and can influence emotional and spiritual well-being.

1 Corinthians 6:16 (NIV) - "Do you not know that he who unites himself with a prostitute is one with her in body? For it is said, 'The two will become one flesh.'"

Impact of Sexual Sin

Engaging in sexual sin can lead to the formation of unhealthy soul ties, binding individuals in ways they might not anticipate. This can result in emotional entanglements, spiritual turmoil, and a distortion of one's sense of self. The consequences often extend far beyond the immediate physical act.

Galatians 5:19-21 (NIV) - "The acts of the flesh are obvious: sexual immorality, impurity, and debauchery... I warn you, as I did before, that those who live like this will not inherit the kingdom of God."

Redemption and Healing

Fortunately, the grace and mercy of God extend even to those ensnared by sexual sin and its repercussions. Through repentance, seeking forgiveness, and committing to purity, individuals can find healing and restoration.

1 John 1:9 (NIV) - "If we confess our sins, he is faithful and just and will forgive us our sins and purify us from all unrighteousness."

Conclusion

The issue of soul ties and sexual sin is complex and deeply impactful. The scriptures warn against such behaviors and offer a path to redemption and healing. By embracing the teachings of the Bible, individuals can break free from these entanglements and pursue spiritual and emotional restoration.